A-Z music celebration
Coloring and Activity book

Nonku Kunene Adumetey

Illustrated by Oksana Panomar

Aa

A A A A A A A A

a a a a a a a a

African drum

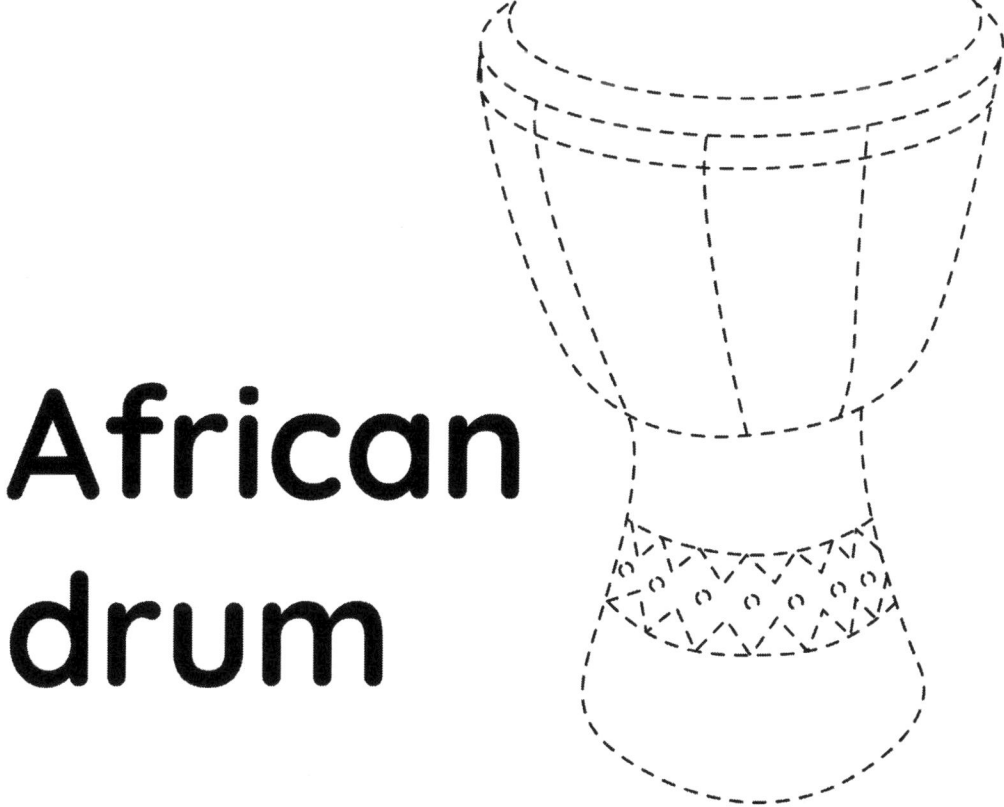

Bb

Ballet

Bb

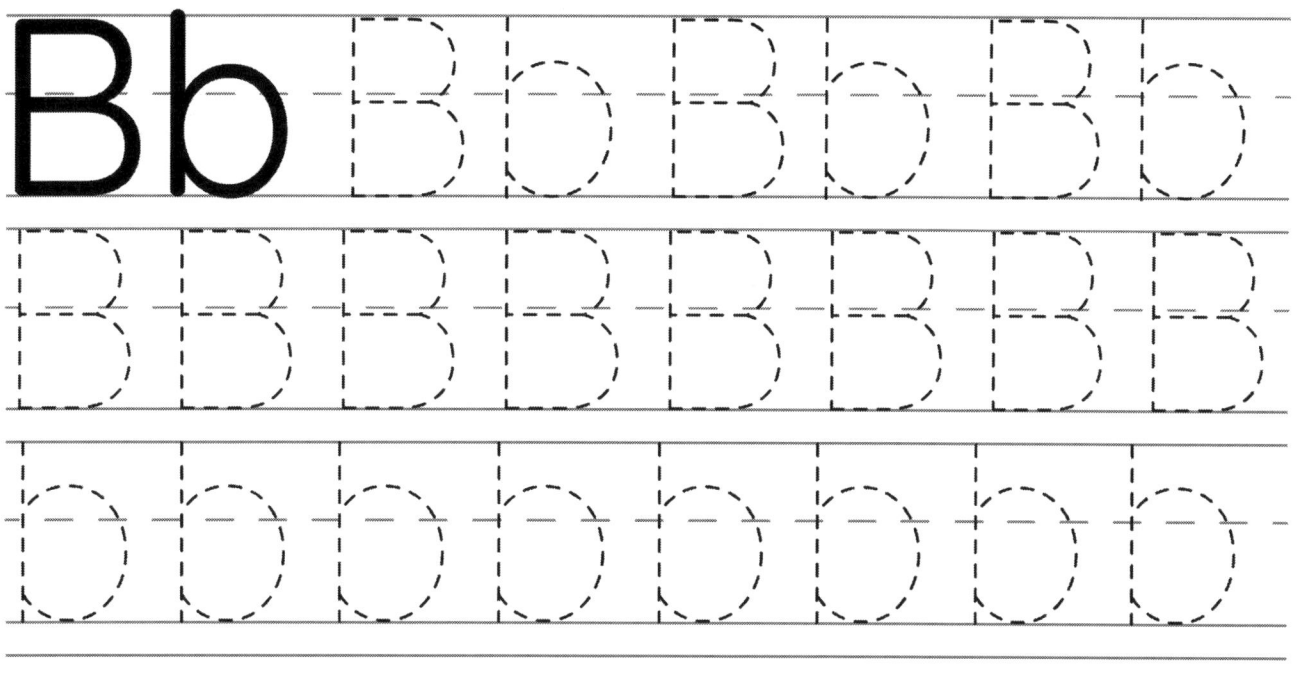

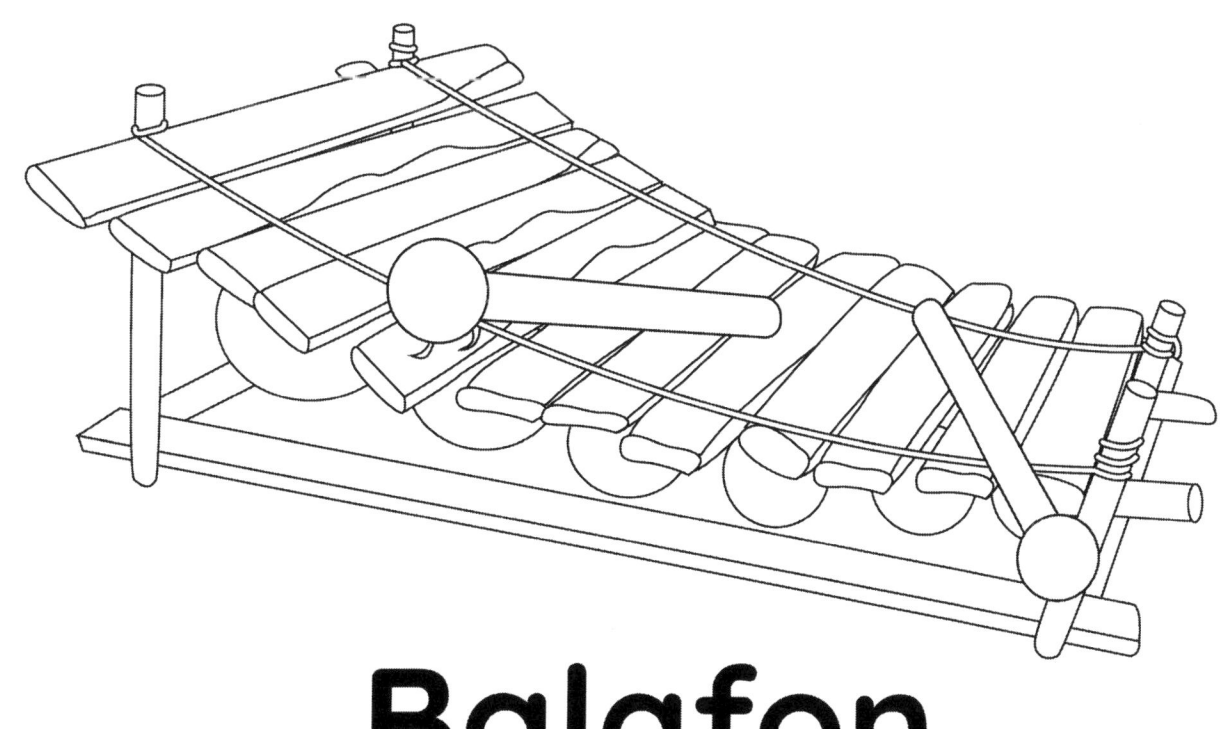

Balafon

Cc

Calabash Shaker

Cello

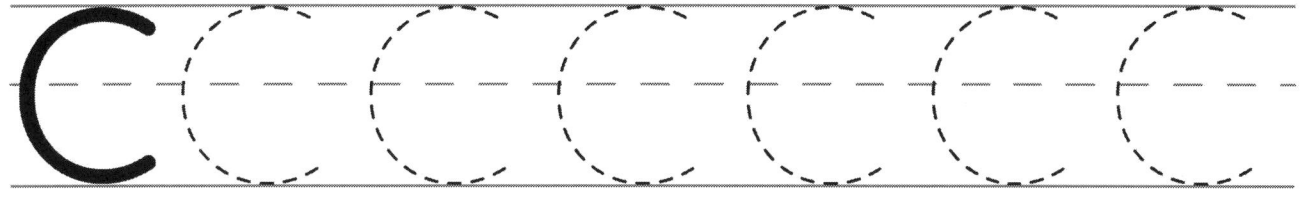

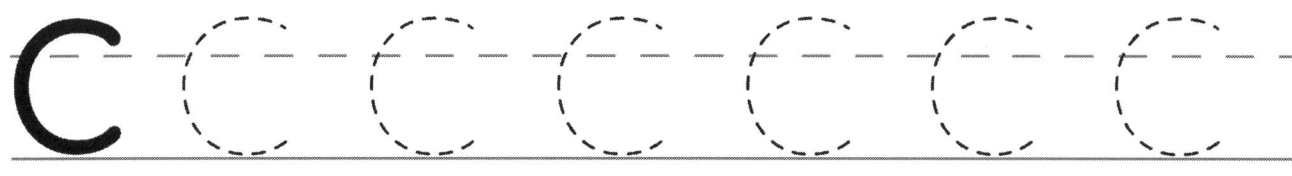

Trace and color the Cello

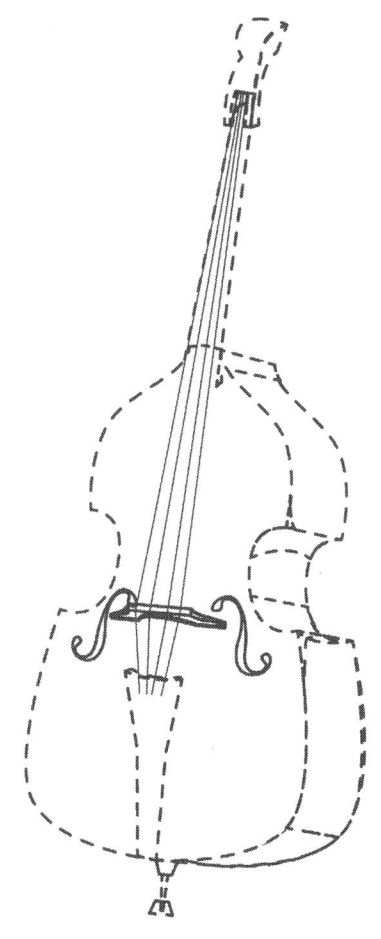

Dd

Dance

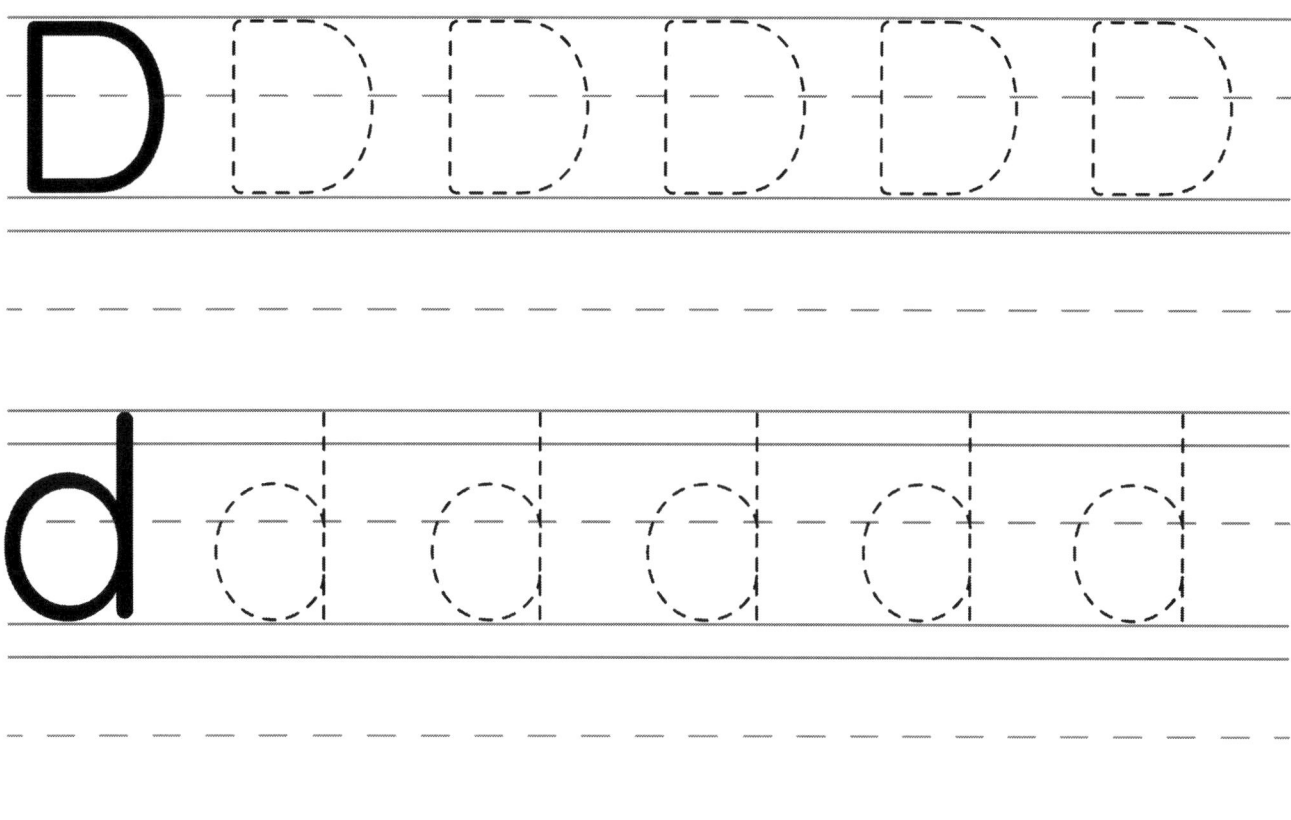

Do you like to dance?_____

What is your favorite song? _____

What is your favorite dance?_____

It's time for a dance party! Play your favorite song and dance with family and friends.

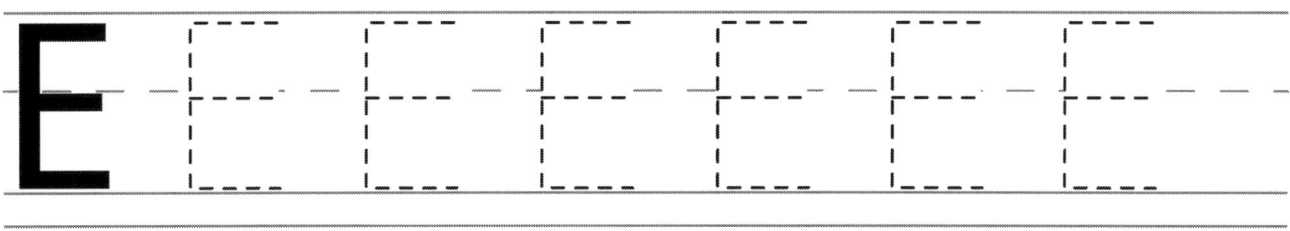

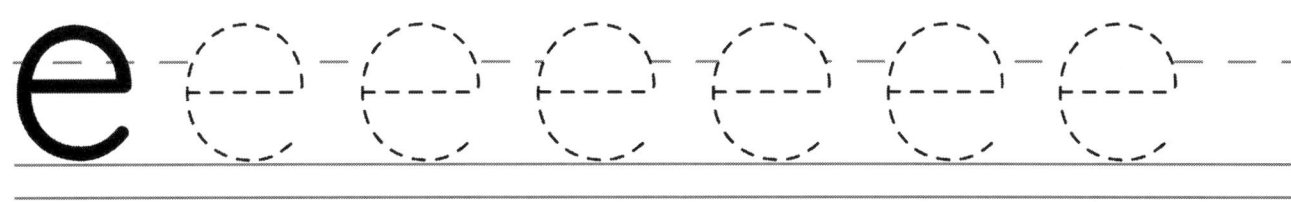

Ff

Flamenco

Gg

Guitar

Gg

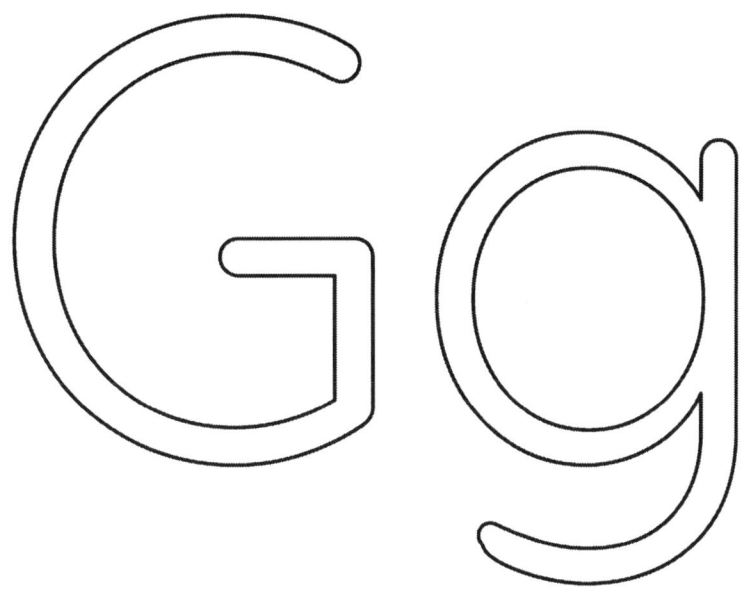

Trace and color the gumboot.

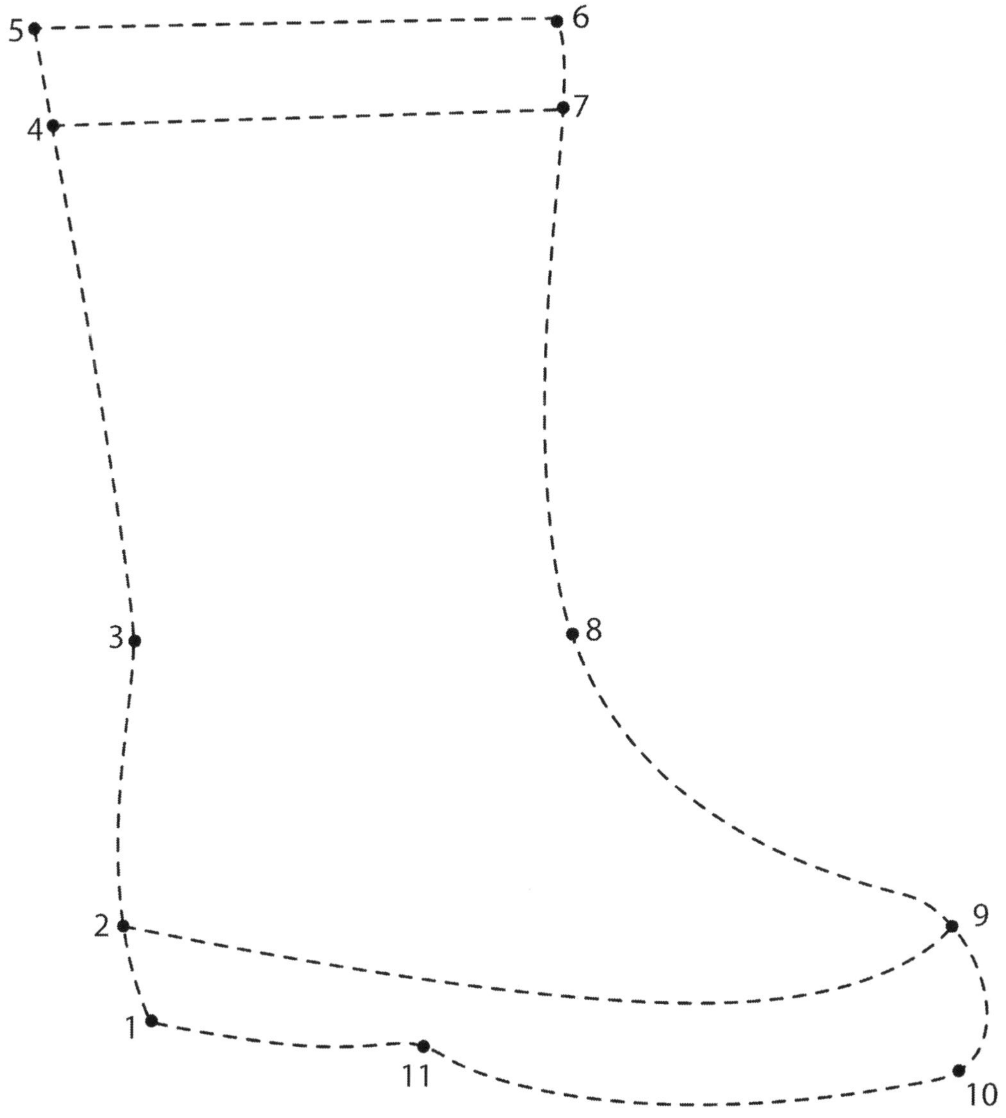

Harp

Hh

Hira gasy:
A musical tradition in Madagascar

Jj

Trace and Color the jingle bell.

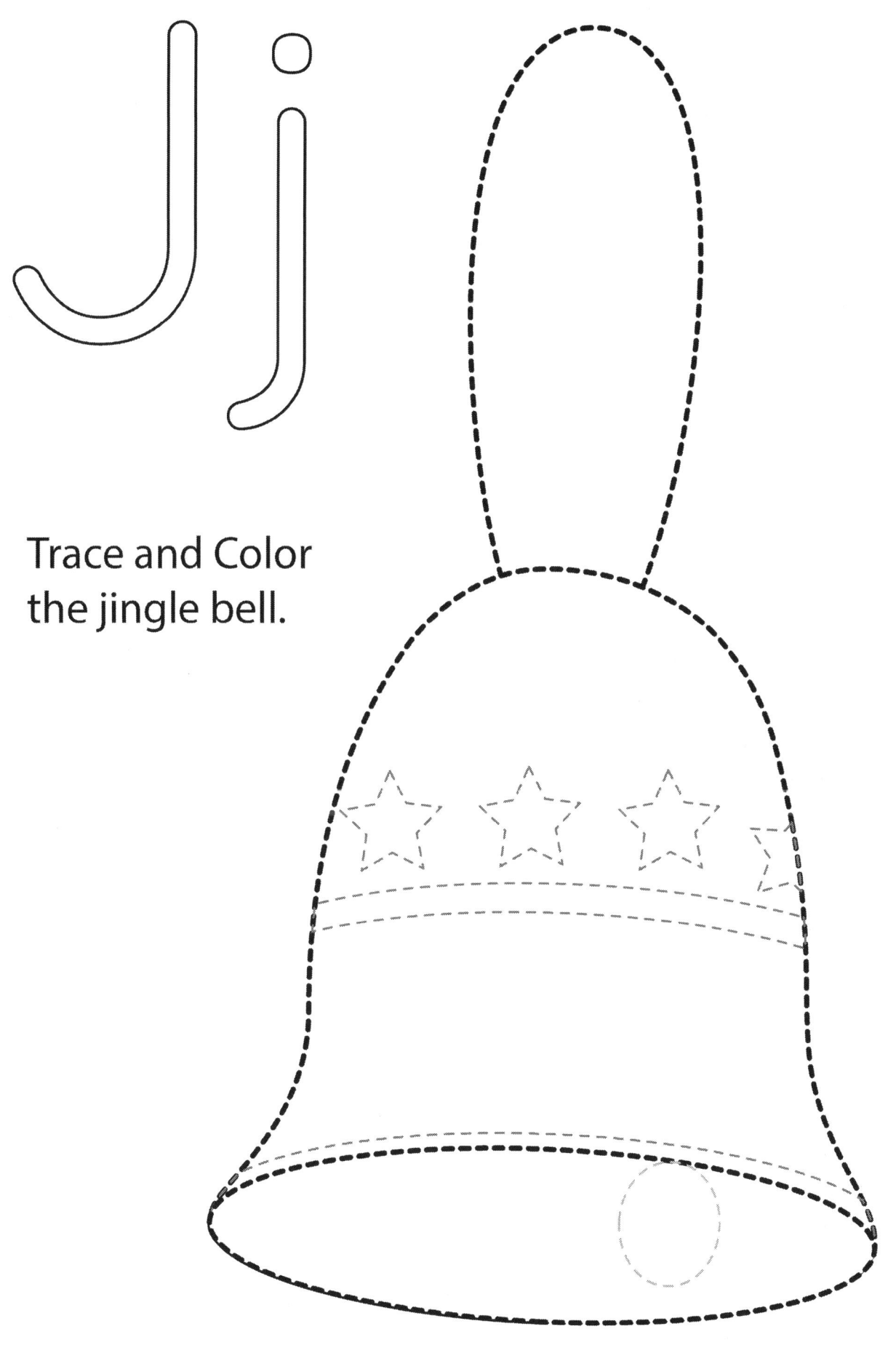

Kk

Kk

Kebero Drum:
Originating from Ethiopia.

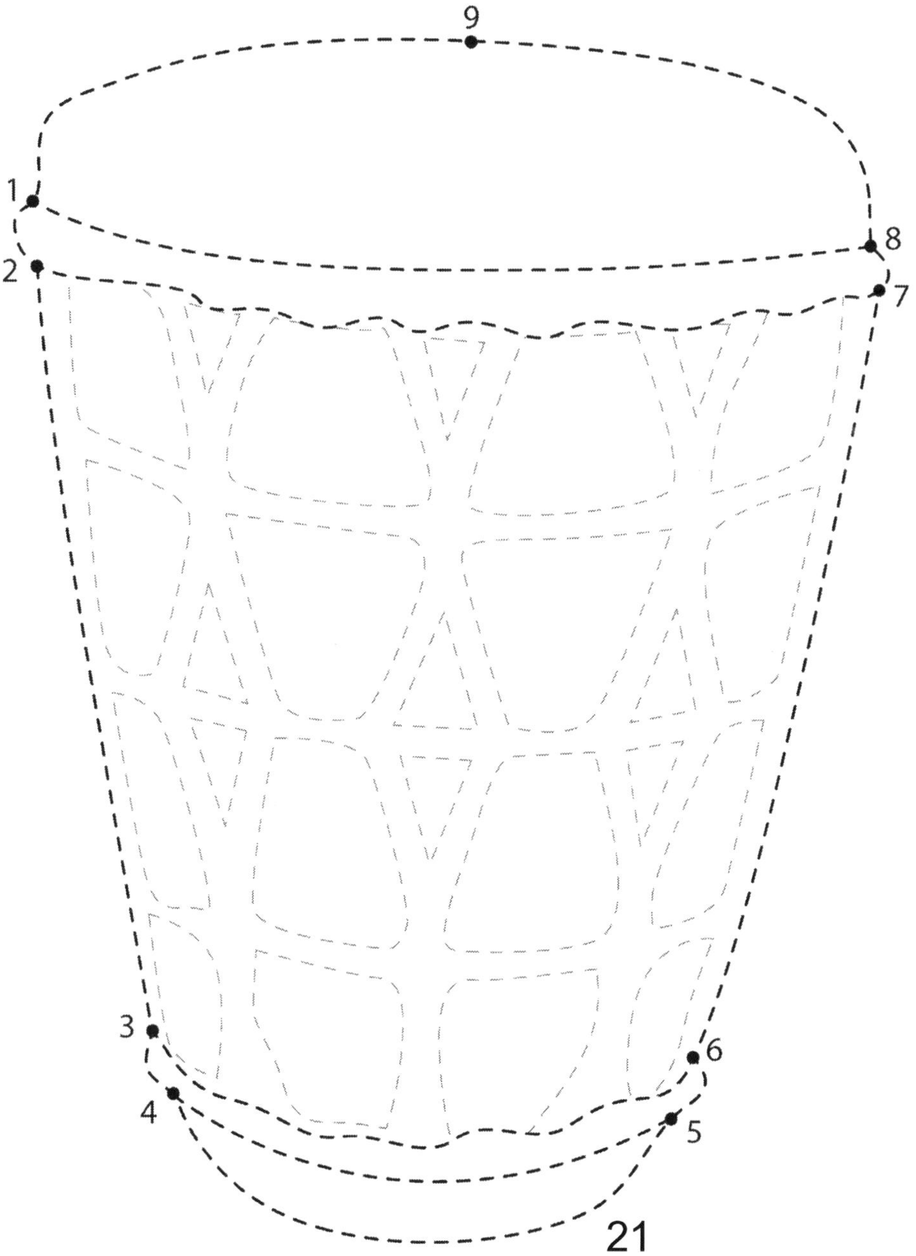

Ll

Lunga Drum: Commonly used in West Africa.

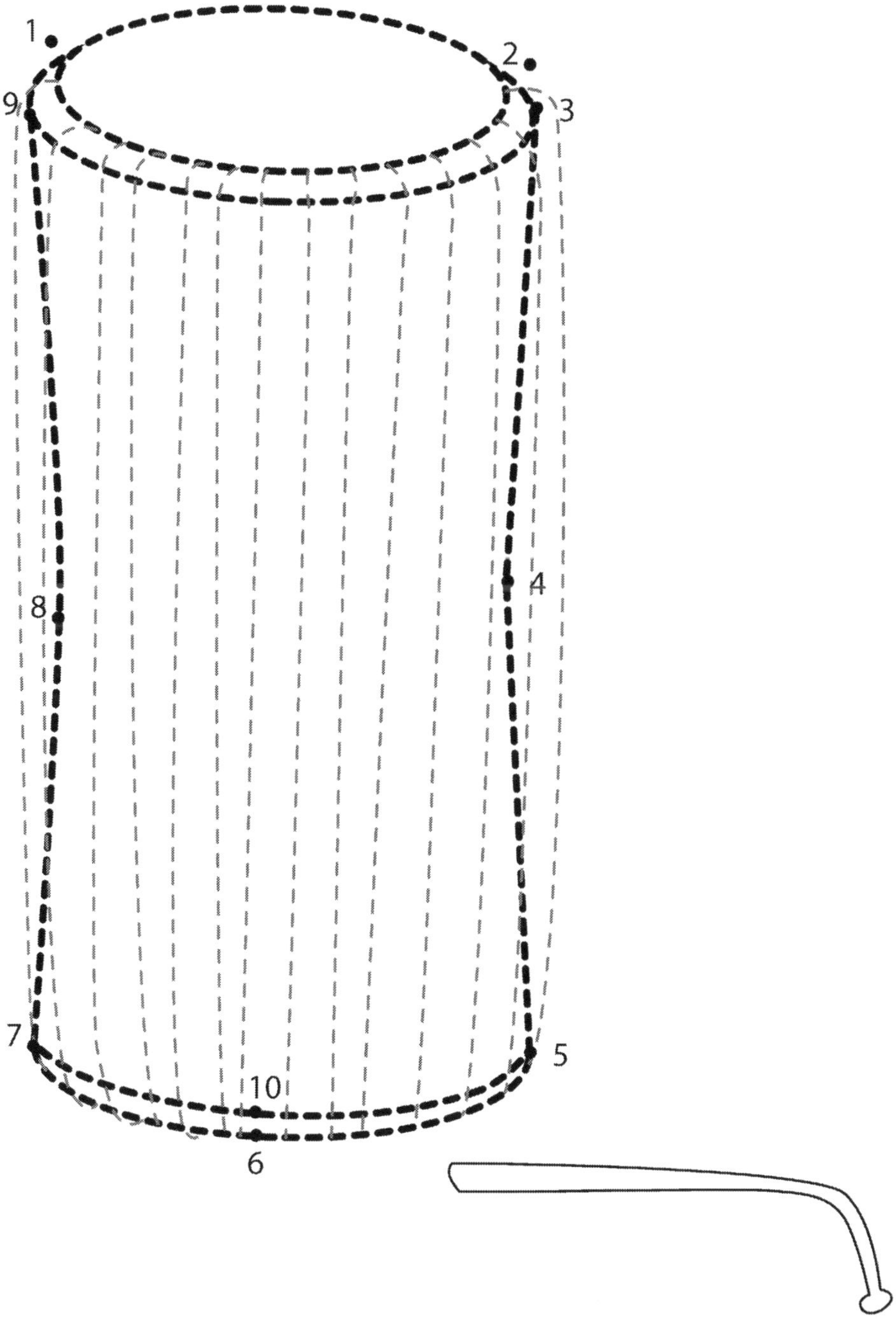

23

Mm

Marimba

Mm

Marimba sticks are called mallets. Color and match the mallets.

Nn

Nn

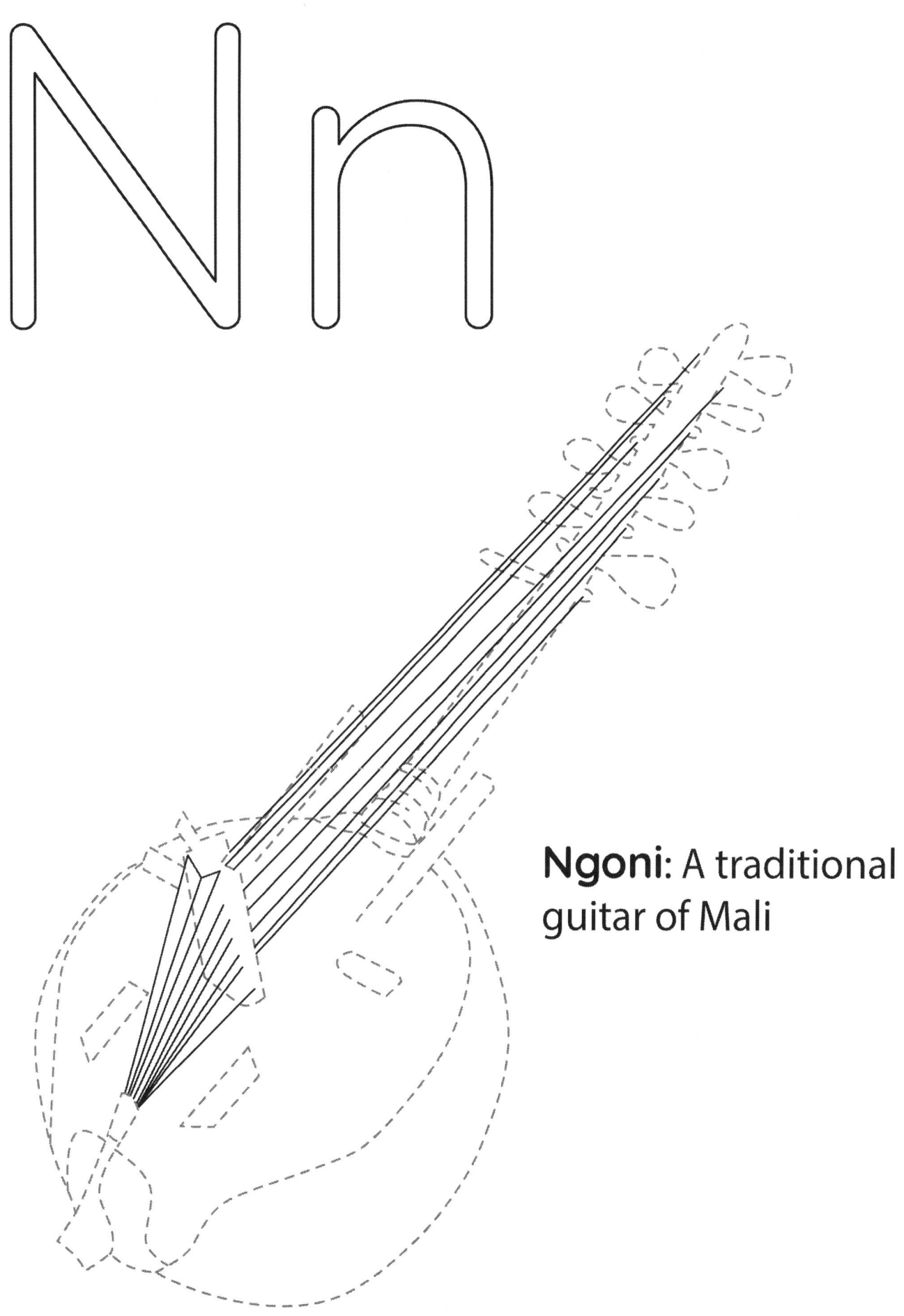

Ngoni: A traditional guitar of Mali

Oo Organ

I am

Loved.

I am

kind.

I am

joyful.

Can you guess the seasons?

I am

important.

I am

brave.

I am

unique.

My Voice

Matters!

33

I am not

afraid of a

challenge.

I

matter!

I can make

a difference.

I believe

in myself.

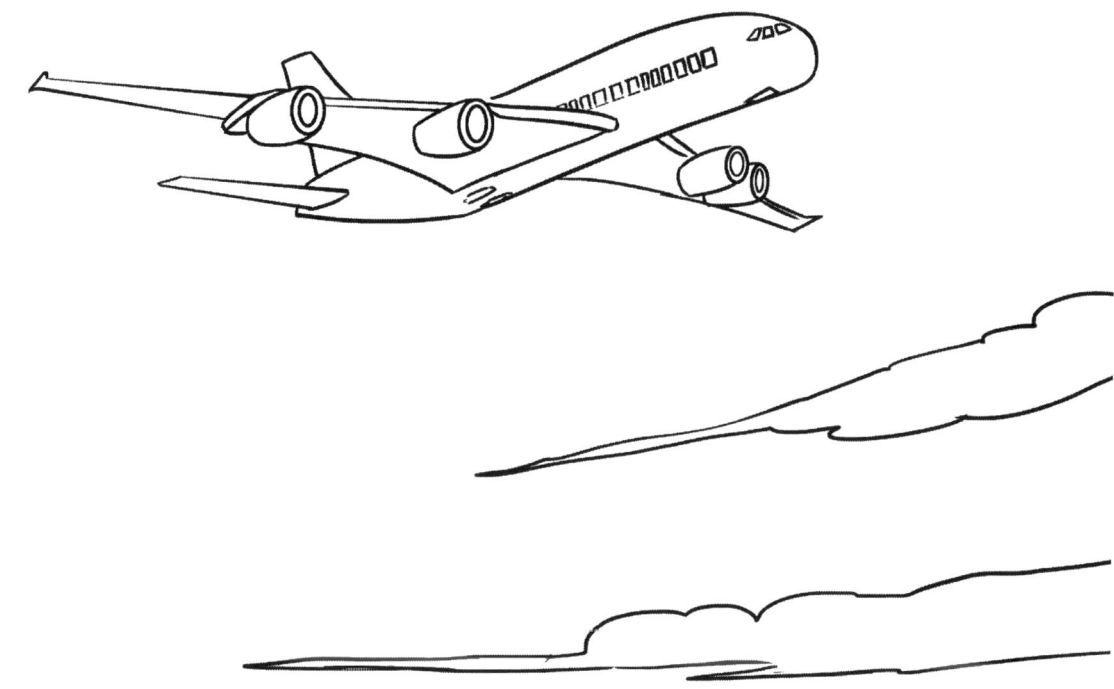

Trace and color this page

My voice is bold

My Voice is my

superpower.

What is your voice?

___

How do you celebrate it?

___

Draw what your voice means to you.

NONKU'S CORNER

I Celebrate My Voice - Coloring and Affirmations Book
© Copyright 2022 Nonku Kunene Adumetey
All rights reserved

Author:
Nonku Kunene Adumetey

Illustrator:
Mary K. Biswas

Published 2022

ISBN: 978-1-7378957-0-1

www.nonkuscorner.com

Made in the USA
Las Vegas, NV
15 February 2022